CAMBRIDGE ENGLISH
Worldwide
Starter Listening and Speaking Pack

ANDREW LITTLEJOHN & DIANA HICKS

CAMBRIDGE
UNIVERSITY PRESS

PUBLISHED BY THE PRESS SYNDICATE OF THE UNIVERSITY OF CAMBRIDGE
The Pitt Building, Trumpington Street, Cambridge CB2 1RP, United Kingdom

CAMBRIDGE UNIVERSITY PRESS
The Edinburgh Building, Cambridge CB2 2RU, United Kingdom
40 West 20th Street, New York, NY 10011-4211, USA
10 Stamford Road, Oakleigh, Melbourne 3166, Australia

First published 1999

Printed in the United Kingdom at the University Press, Cambridge.

ISBN 0 521 64513 1 Listening and Speaking Pack
ISBN 0 521 64517 4 Student's Book
ISBN 0 521 64516 6 Workbook
ISBN 0 521 64515 8 Teacher's Book
ISBN 0 521 64514 X Class Cassette Set

Contents

1 Learn English!

---

1 The alphabet

The alphabet

1.1 🔲 Listen and say

ABC DEF GHI JKL MNO PQRS TUV WXYZ

1.2 Listen and write

🔲 Listen. Write the letters.

1 F _ _ _ B _ _ _ 2 S _ _ D _ _ _ _ 3 B _ _ 4 T _ _ _ _ _ _ _ N _ 5 T _ _ _ 6 H _ _ _ _ _

Write the words.

a ⚽ football   b ☎   c 🚗   d 🏛 h   e 🥪   f 🚌

---

2 Talk to Tom

Writing and speaking

Write your answers.

TOM: Hello.

YOU: ....

TOM: How are you?

YOU: ....

TOM: I'm fine. Good. Here's my bus. Bye!

YOU: ....

🔲 Talk to Tom on the cassette.

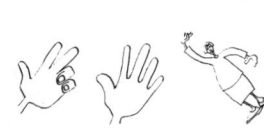

---

3 Sing a song! Hello, friend (How are you?)

🔲 Listen and sing 'Hello, friend (How are you?)'.
The words are on page 88 in your Student's Book.

Topic 2 **Around the world**

---

1 **Learn some sentences**

Listen and repeat

Listen and say the sentences.

Speak English.	Hello.
Read.	How are you?
Listen.	Fine, thanks.
Write.	How are you?

---

2 **Listen and tick**

Numbers

Listen and tick (✓) the number.

a 2 ☐ 12 ☐ c 4 ☐ 14 ☐ e 3 ☐ 13 ☐

b 6 ☐ 16 ☐ d 8 ☐ 11 ☐ f 5 ☐ 15 ☐

---

3 **Talk to Cathy**

Writing and speaking

Write your answers to Cathy's questions.

CATHY: Hello. What's your name?

YOU: ....

CATHY: My name's Cathy. How are you?

YOU: ....

CATHY: I'm fine. I'm from Scotland. Where are you from?

YOU: ....

CATHY: That's interesting. Is your town big or small?

YOU: ....

CATHY: I'm from Edinburgh. Edinburgh is a big city. See you later! Bye!

YOU: ....

Now talk to Cathy on the cassette.

4 Learn some sentences

Listen and repeat

Listen and say the sentences.

My name's Jack.	This is Marek.
I'm eleven years old.	He's thirteen years old.
This is Carolina.	What's your name?
She's twelve years old.	How old are you?

5 Say it clearly!

/tiːn/ *thirteen* /ti/ *thirty*

5.1 Say the numbers

Listen and say the numbers.

13 thirteen	30 thirty	14 fourteen	40 forty	15 fifteen
50 fifty	16 sixteen	60 sixty	17 seventeen	70 seventy
18 eighteen	80 eighty	19 nineteen	90 ninety	

5.2 What number is it?

Listen. Write the numbers.

a ....   b ....   c ....

d ....   e ....   f ....

6 Sing a song! Hello, hello!

Listen and sing 'Hello, hello!'.
The words are on page 88
in your Student's Book.

Language focus

1 Talk to Tom

Writing and speaking

Write your answers to Tom's questions.

TOM: Hello. My name's Tom. What's your name?

YOU: ....

TOM: Where are you from?

YOU: ....

TOM: Oh. I'm from England. What class are you in at school?

YOU: ....

TOM: I'm in Class 2. My school is in London. Where is your school?

YOU: ....

TOM: That's interesting. See you soon! Bye!

YOU: ....

Now talk to Tom on the cassette.

2 Say it clearly!

Personal pronouns

2.1 Listen and say

Listen and say the words.

I'm	I'm from England.	You're	You're in Class 2.	She's	She's from Italy.
You're	You're in Class 1.	They're	They're from Brazil.	It's	It's in my bag.
We're	We're in school.	He's	He's in Brazil.	It's	It's in my bag.

2.2 Listen and write

Listen. Write about Simon and Mari.

Name: Simon   Mari

From: ....

Age: ....

Class: ....

Extension

For more work on Unit 3, see Extension Exercises 1 and 2 on page 19.

4 Topic Your country

1 Talk to Cathy

Writing and speaking

Write your answers to Cathy's questions.

CATHY: Hello. How are you?

YOU: ....

CATHY: I'm fine. Tell me about your country. Is it very big?

YOU: ....

CATHY: My country is Scotland. It has got mountains and rivers. What about your country?

YOU: ....

CATHY: Scotland has got beaches, too. What about your country?

YOU: ....

CATHY: We speak English in Scotland. What is your language?

YOU: ....

CATHY: Your English is very good! See you later. Bye!

YOU: ....

▭ Now talk to Cathy on the cassette.

2 Say it clearly!

Vowels

▭ Listen and say.

/ɪ/ Spanish Polish Turkish Italian   /e/ French
/iː/ Portuguese Japanese Chinese Greek   /æ/ Arabic
In Spain, they speak Spanish.
In Brazil, they speak Portuguese.

3 Sing a song! There is a country

▭ Listen and sing 'There is a country'.
The words are on page 88 in your Student's Book.

Extension

For more work on Unit 4, see Extension Exercise 3 on page 19.

5 Language focus

1 Talk to Tom

Writing and speaking

Write your answers to Tom's questions.

TOM: Hello again! How are you?

YOU: ....

TOM: I'm fine. Tell me, where is your house?

YOU: ....

TOM: My house is in London. Is your house very big?

YOU: ....

TOM: My house is small. It has got two bedrooms. What about your house?

YOU: ....

TOM: My bedroom is a big room. It's a nice room. Is your bedroom big?

YOU: ....

TOM: That's interesting. See you soon. Bye!

YOU: ....

Now talk to Tom on the cassette.

2 Learn some sentences

Listen and repeat

Listen and say the sentences.

This is my house.	Can I have this magazine, please?
This is the living room.	That's 50 pence, please.
That's the bathroom.	Here you are.
Come upstairs.	Thank you.

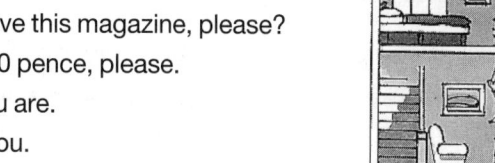

3 Say it clearly!

/s/ /z/ /ɪz/

Listen and say the words.

/s/ plants books   /z/ pictures radios chairs   /ɪz/ oranges exercises

Extension

For more work on Unit 5, see Extension Exercise 4 on page 20.

Topic Animal facts

1 Talk to Tom

Writing and speaking

Write your answers to Tom's questions.

TOM: Hello.

YOU: ....

TOM: How are you?

YOU: ....

TOM: I'm fine. I like playing the guitar. Can you play the guitar?

YOU: ....

TOM: Can you play other musical instruments?

YOU: ....

TOM: What about sports?

YOU: ....

TOM: Well, I go swimming every day. Can you swim?

YOU: ....

TOM: We can go swimming together! What's your telephone number?

YOU: ....

TOM: I can talk to you later. Bye!

YOU: ....

Now talk to Tom on the cassette.

2 Say it clearly!

/æ/ *can, kangaroo*

Listen and say the words and sentences. Open your mouth!

animal apple bag can cat flat kangaroo
man sandwich thanks that has

That man has an apple in his bag.
Kangaroos and cats are animals.
The sandwich is in that bag.

3 Sing a song! I can't do what a toucan can

Listen and sing 'I can't do what a toucan can'.

The words are on page 88 in your Student's Book.

Extension

For more work on Unit 6, see Extension Exercise 5 on page 20.

7 Language focus

---

1 Say it clearly!

Syllables

1.1 International words

 Listen and say the words on the cassette.

Words with one syllable: film jeans club

Words with two syllables: taxi football café cassette

Words with three syllables: dictionary radio
telephone computer cinema sandwiches

1.2 Some more words

 Listen and say the words. Put the words in the correct circle.

pen cassette kangaroo school classroom woman friends Africa pencil
toucan zebra umbrella picture plant chair table tiger

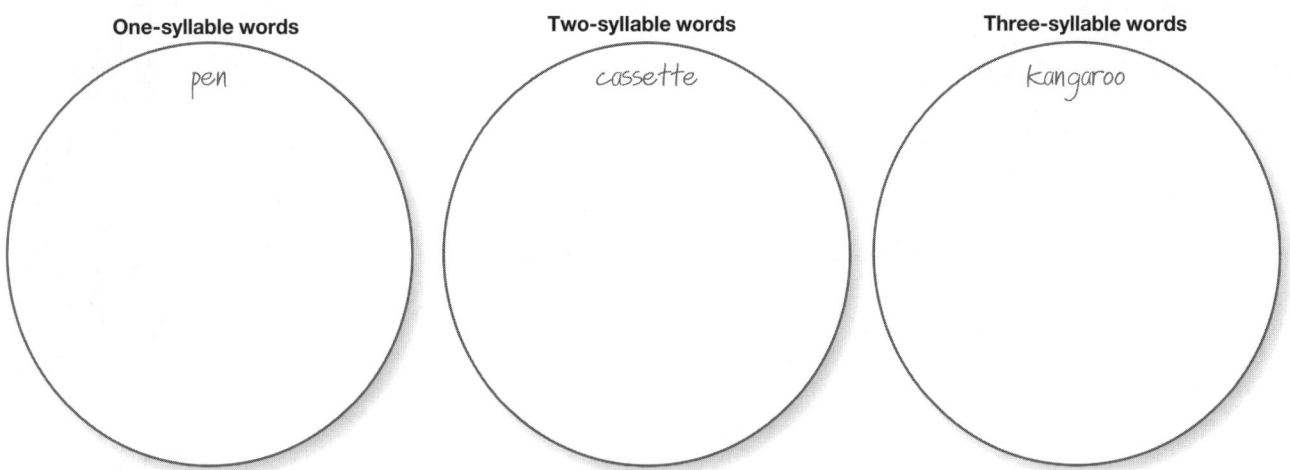

One-syllable words

pen

Two-syllable words

cassette

Three-syllable words

kangaroo

Look at Units 1–6 in your Student's Book. Write three more words in each circle.

---

2 Learn some sentences

Listen and repeat

 Listen and say the sentences.

What's 'spaghetti' in English? Can I have a dictionary, please?
What does 'taxi' mean? Can you play the cassette again, please?
I don't understand this word. Can you say that again, please?

Extension

For more work on Unit 7, see Extension Exercises 6 and 7 on pages 20 and 21.

8 Topic Natural food

1 Learn some sentences

Listen and say the sentences.

A polar bear eats meat.
A fish eats meat and plants.
A penguin eats fish.

The birdwing butterfly is a very big butterfly.
It is also very beautiful.
It lives in forests.
It eats flowers.

2 Talk to Tom

Speaking and writing

Write your answers to Tom's questions.

TOM: Hello. How are you?

YOU: ....

TOM: I'm fine. Can you help me with my homework? It's about food chains.

YOU: ....

TOM: I know a polar bear eats seals. What about a seal?

YOU: ....

....

TOM: And a fish?

YOU: ....

....

TOM: Oh, that's right. Now, what about a snake?

YOU: ....

....

TOM: And a frog?

YOU: ....

TOM: That's all. Thanks very much! Bye!

YOU: ....

📼 Now talk to Tom on the cassette.

3   Say it clearly!

's': /s/, /z/ and /ɪz/

📼 There are three ways to say 's'. Listen. Say the words and sentences.

/s/: eats   puts   plants

/z/: is   lives   flies   comes   frogs   snails   butterflies

/ɪz/: changes   fishes

A frog eats [s] snails [z].

A caterpillar comes [z] from an egg.

Butterflies [z] fly in the forest.

A caterpillar changes [ɪz] into a butterfly.

Fishes [ɪz] eat plants [s].

4   Sing a song!   There's an animal in my pocket

📼 Listen and sing 'There's an animal in my pocket'.

The words are on page 89 in your Student's Book.

9 Language focus

Present simple; 'there is'/
'there are'; in the shops

1 Learn some sentences

Listen and repeat

Listen and say the sentences.

This is my pet.   There are seven continents in the world.
He lives in my house.   There are 180 countries in the world.
He sleeps eight hours every day.   There is a very long river in Egypt.
He eats meat.   There is a very big forest in Brazil.

2 Talk to Tom

Writing, listening and speaking

Write your answers to Tom's questions.

TOM: Hello.

YOU: ....

TOM: How are you?

YOU: ....

TOM: I'm fine. Have you got a pet?

YOU: ....

TOM: Oh. I've got a pet. It's a parrot. She can talk. Say hello to Polly.

YOU: ....

POLLY: Hello.

TOM: Polly comes from South America. Where are you from?

YOU: ....

TOM: Oh. Have a lot of people got pets in your country?

YOU: ....

TOM: What pets have they got?

YOU: ....

TOM: That's interesting. I can talk to you again soon. Bye!

YOU: ....

You can talk to Tom on the cassette.

Extension

For more work on Unit 9, see Extension Exercise 8 on page 21.

Topic 10 The clothes we wear

---

1 Talk to Cathy

Writing and speaking

Write your answers to Cathy's questions.

CATHY: Hello, how are you?

YOU: ....

CATHY: I'm fine. I've got a new sweater. It's winter here now. Is it winter in your country?

YOU: ....

CATHY: When is it warm?

YOU: ....

CATHY: That's interesting.

YOU: ....

CATHY: When is it windy?

YOU: ....

CATHY: Oh. It's windy in November in Britain. It's also wet. When is it wet in your country?

YOU: ....

CATHY: Oh dear! I can talk to you again later. Bye!

YOU: ....

Now talk to Cathy on the cassette.

---

2 Say it clearly!

/w/

Listen. Say the words and sentences.

walk windy wet warm	In winter, the weather is wet.
winter wear weather	We wear warm clothes in the winter.
	It is windy weather today.

---

3 Sing a song! Go south, go north!

Listen and sing 'Go south, go north!'.
The words are on page 89 in your Student's Book.

Language focus

1 Talk to Tom

Writing and speaking

🔲 Write your answers to Tom's questions. Then talk to him on the cassette.

TOM: Hello. How are you?

YOU: ....

TOM: I'm fine. It's very hot here today. Is it hot in your country?

YOU: ....

TOM: It's summer here. Is it summer in your country?

YOU: ....

TOM: It's 25 degrees today. What temperature is it with you?

YOU: ....

TOM: Oh. At school we can wear shorts and T-shirts. What can you wear at school?

YOU: ....

TOM: We can go to a swimming pool after school. Can you go to a swimming pool in your town?

YOU: ....

TOM: I've got a lot of homework now. I can talk to you again soon. Bye.

YOU: ....

2 Say it clearly!

/s/ and /z/

2.1 Say the words

🔲 Listen. Say the words.

/s/ it's   that's   this   months   students   shorts   dress
/z/ she's   he's   Susan's   mother's   days   years   clothes   shoes   sandals   gloves   colours   trousers

2.2 Listen and write

🔲 Listen. Write the words in the lists.

fireworks   coats   thanks   animals   class   holidays   friends   shoes   bus   countries   weeks   trees

/s/ sound   *fireworks*   /z/ sound   *animals*

Extension

For more work on Unit 11, see Extension Exercise 9 on page 22.

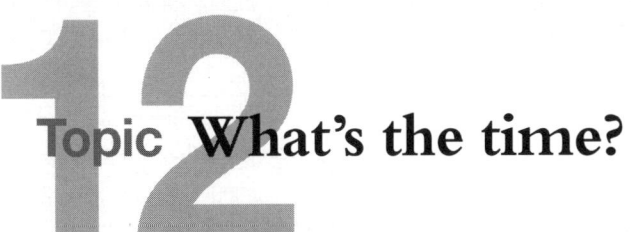

Topic 12 What's the time?

1 Talk to Cathy

Writing and speaking

Write your answers to Cathy's questions.

CATHY: Hello. How are you?

YOU: ....

CATHY: I'm fine. It's a sunny day here. Is it sunny where you are?

YOU: ....

CATHY: I can go to the park today. Is there a park near you?

YOU: ....

CATHY: Oh. I can ride my bicycle in the park. Can you ride a bicycle?

YOU: ....

CATHY: What can you do on a sunny day where you live?

YOU: ....

CATHY: That's interesting. Where can you walk?

YOU: ....

CATHY: I can walk in the mountains in Scotland. They're beautiful! Are there mountains near you?

YOU: ....

CATHY: I can talk to you again later. Bye!

YOU: ....

Now talk to Cathy on the cassette.

2 Say it clearly!

'-s'

Remember the '-s'! Listen. Say the words and sentences.

comes	The sun comes up at 6 o'clock.	eats	He eats at 1 o'clock.
goes	The sun goes down at 7 o'clock.	plays	He plays basketball at school.
gets	Simon gets up at 7 o'clock.		

3 Sing a song! Round and round

Listen and sing 'Round and round'.
The words are on page 89 in your Student's Book.

Language focus

---

1 Say it clearly!

' 've got', ' 's got'

 Listen and say the words and sentences.

I've got	I've got a new pet.	He's got	He's got a small house.
You've got	You've got a test tomorrow.	She's got	She's got a big flat.
We've got	We've got a present for you.	It's got	It's got three bedrooms.
They've got	They've got a lot of pets.		

---

2 Listen and write

 Listen. Draw lines to the correct things.

Simon

Marie

Lee

  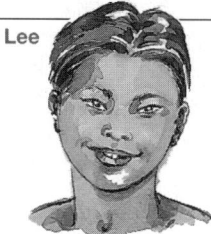

three kittens   **four kittens**   **five kittens**   **two bedrooms**   **three bedrooms**   **four bedrooms**

   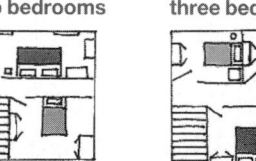 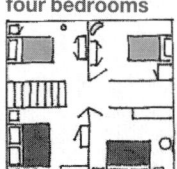

Write about Lee.

Lee's got a flat.

It's got ....

He's got ....

---

3 In the classroom

Listen and repeat

 Listen and say the sentences.

What page are we on?   What's for homework?   I can't find my book.

Sorry, I can't hear the cassette.   I don't understand this exercise.

Extension

For more work on Unit 13, see Extension Exercise 10 on page 22.

Extension exercises

1 Unit 3
This or that?

Listen and write

Listen to the cassette. Write the word in the correct circle.

house   computer   radio   school
book   football   cassette   televison

'this'

'that'

2 Unit 3
Where are they from?

Listen and match

Listen. Match the names and the places.

Susi ——————————— Poland

Konrad —————— Japan

Shoko and Yoshi ——— the USA

Anali ——— Colombia

Tim and Dave ——— Brazil

3 Unit 4
This country ...

Listen and write

Listen and complete the text.

Great Britain

This country .... in Europe. They speak English ....
52 million people .... there.

Mexico

This country is .... North America. They speak ....
there. It has got ...., rivers, forests and beaches.

India

This country is in .... It is very, very .... 850 million
.... live there. They speak Hindi, English and 14 more .... there.

Japan

This .... is in Asia. It has got a very big .... They ....
Japanese there.

The Vatican

.... country is in Europe. It is very, very ....
1000 .... live there. They speak .... and Latin.

4　Unit 5
True or false?

 Listen. Write 'true' or 'false'.

1　Monica is in the kitchen. *true*

2　Len is in the kitchen. ....

3　Sally and Anne are in the bedroom. ....

4　Colin is in the park. ....

5　Bill is in the park. ....

6　The person on the telephone is in bed. ....

5　Unit 6
What can chimpanzees do?

 Listen and complete the chart.

Chimpanzees	
can	can't

6　Unit 7
Flamingos

Read about flamingos.

> Flamingos come from many countries. They are pink in colour. They have long legs. They live near salt water. They eat fish and they can fly. The nest is near water. It is on the ground. A female flamingo sits on two eggs.

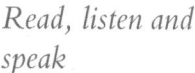 Listen to Cathy. She has a lot of wrong information! Complete the table with the correct information.

	Cathy thinks …	*Correct information*
Flamingo nests		
Colour		
Size		
Nests and water		

Now look at Unit 7 in your Workbook and check your answers.

7   Unit 7
Talk to Cathy

Write your answers to Cathy's questions. Then talk to her on the cassette.

CATHY: Hello! It's sports day at my school today. I'm in the swimming team. Can you swim?

YOU: ....

CATHY: I'm in the basketball team, too. Can you play basketball?

YOU: ....

CATHY: My friend can jump two metres high. Can you jump two metres?

YOU: ....

CATHY: She can also run a kilometre in six minutes. Can you run very fast?

YOU: ....

CATHY: Can you do other sports?

YOU: ....

CATHY: That's interesting. I can talk to you later. Bye!

YOU: ....

8   Unit 9
In the music shop

You are in a shop. Match the sentences to the correct place. Then talk to the assistant on the cassette.

1 Thank you. How much is that?   3 Can I have the free song book, please?

2 Thank you. Bye.   4 Here's £10.

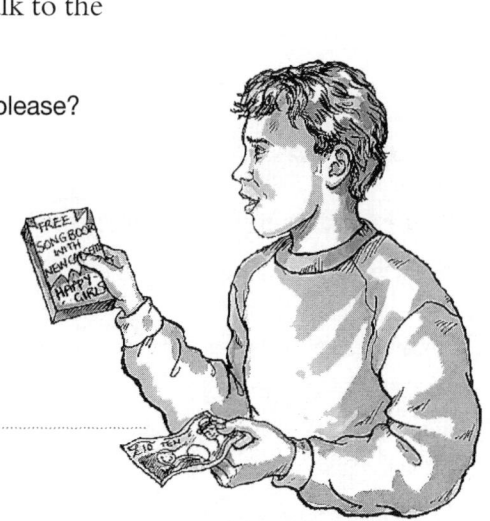

JIM: Can I have the new *Happy Girls* cassette, please?

ASSISTANT: Yes, here it is.

JIM: Thank you, er ...

ASSISTANT: Is that OK?

JIM: ....

ASSISTANT: Oh. Sorry. Here you are.

JIM: ....

ASSISTANT: That's £7 please.

JIM: ....

ASSISTANT: Thanks. Here you are. £3 change.

JIM: ....

ASSISTANT: Bye.

At the carnival!

📇 Listen and follow the conversation.
Then cover Susan's part and talk to Tony.
(Use the 'pause' button on your cassette player.)

TONY: Hello.

SUSAN: Hello, Tony. It's Susan.

TONY: Hi, Susan.

SUSAN: Listen. Do you want to come to the carnival tomorrow?

TONY: Tomorrow? That's Saturday.

SUSAN: That's right. Can you come?

TONY: Fantastic! Yes, I can come. What time?

SUSAN: The carnival starts at 6 o'clock.

TONY: Where can we meet?

SUSAN: At my house!

TONY: OK. Six o'clock at your house. Fine. Bye!

SUSAN: Bye.

Jack's week

📇 Listen and complete the information.

Jack …	Day	Time
goes to school	Monday to Friday	9.00 to 3.30
plays football		
swims		
has a guitar lesson		
has a piano lesson		
goes to bed		
goes to his grandmother's house		

Acknowledgements

The authors and publishers are grateful to the following illustrators:

Illustrators: Sophie Allington: pp. 12 *t* & *b*, 13 *t*; Gecko Limited: all DTP illustrations and graphics; Peter Kent: p.4 *m*; Doreen McGuiness: p. 20 *t*; Jenny Norton: p.16; Liz Roberts: pp. 4 *m*, 5 *b*, 7, 8 *t*, 9 *t*, 10 *t*, 12 *m*, 14, 15 *t*, 16, 17 *t*, 18 *b*, 19 *m*, 20 *b*, 21, 22; Debbie Ryder: pp. 4 *b*, 6 *b*, 8 *b*, 10 *b*, 13 *b*, 15 *b*, 17 *b*; John Storey: p. 5 *t*.

t = top *m* = middle *b* = bottom *l* = left *r* = right

Cover design by Dunne & Scully based on an illustration by Felicity Roma Bowers.

Sound recordings by Martin Williamson, Prolingua Productions at Studio AVP.

Freelance editorial work by Merideth Levy and Helena Gomm.

Design and production by Gecko Ltd, Bicester, Oxon.